PATRIOTIC AND SENTIMENTAL VERSES

It takes time to write down what you feel about certain situations putting everyday thoughts into verses that are meaningful and resonate with different groups of people.

Stephen is particularly passionate about the plight of displaced people and refugees who are suffering because of war, discrimination, terrorism and other forms of oppression.

His verses are very patriotic portraying the courage and suffering of those who have fought and died for our country. It is with honor and respect that he pays homage in his verses to our fallen heroes who have made this country a safe place to live.

His personal view is and always will be that all people no matter their religion, colour, race or gender must have the right to exist in an environment that is safe and free from persecution.

THE AUTHOR

The author Stephen Price was born in Colsterworth near Grantham, Lincolnshire.

He is an army veteran who served in the Royal Engineers from 1964 through 1973. After his military service he embarked on a career as a trainer working on international development projects around the world. His career took him to thirteen countries in Africa, Middle East and South East Asia.

For twenty-seven years he owned a small training company in the USA. Retiring in March 2019 he returned to the UK to spend time with his family.

THE ILLUSTRATOR

Dave Bull is a professional illustrator with over thirty five years experience working in the publishing, advertising and marketing industry.

He began scribbling as a child and never stopped. Going on to study art at college and gain a BA (Hons) Degree. Working initially within an advertising agency. He began as a junior creative and ended as the Art Director of the agency. Dave left to work freelance and has been working contantly ever since.

He is one of the UK's most versatile commercial artists. Supplying illustrations for the likes of M&S, Morrisons, The Red Cross, B&Q, Waitrose, Local Authorities, Education Establishments, Book Publishers... right through to private commissions for small business and individuals.

Born in Leicester, Dave now lives and works in the rural countryside of Northumberland.

To see more of Dave's work, visit www.davebull.co.uk

CONTENT

A REFUGEE I AM

I am a refugee I have no place to call home,
I live in a tent or shack wherever I can lay my head down,
Just a number on a board describes who I have become,
I have no name anymore,
My dignity has long gone,
Like so many millions more who share the same fate,
I cry and ask myself what I have done to deserve this,
Politicians visit our camp to see how we live,
They bring their cameras this makes great news,
Nothing changes except time,
My name is Sarah but who cares anymore.

MOTHER'S LOVE

My son, my son, you gave your life for us so that we can live in peace,
I miss you dearly each passing day,
No one knows the pain I endure,
They gave me a medal for your sacrifice,
Is that supposed to make it better for me?
The graveyards are full of sons just like you,
With mothers like me wishing you hadn't gone so soon,
The years go by and I grow old,
For you my son you will never grow old,
May God take care of you until we meet again,
Your loving mother.

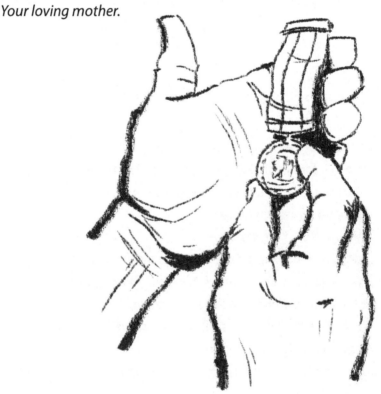

SHED A TEAR

Tears are dry now and years are lost in time,
Time stands still for those who gave their all,
Names are etched in stone in many graveyards around the world,
So, go ahead shed a tear for our fallen heroes,
They shed their blood for you,
No more words to say,
Only memories of the past shown in photos on a wall,
Tears are all that remain to give for those who cry no more,
When they make their final journey home,
A coffin and flag that's all we see,
Their final resting place is here with us,
With loved ones who will take care of them now,
The fresh flowers on their grave says they are finally home to stay.

A MOTHER'S BROKEN DREAMS

There are no winners in war,
Just broken lives and lost dreams,
My children were lost in the rubble when the bomb went off,
In pools of blood they lay no more fear of evil for them,
Robbed of life so soon they never had a chance to grow up.
General, you send your military might to kill the enemy,
My children have no guns to point at you,
So, why do you kill and maim them?
We have nowhere to hide from your planes and bombs,
Lie down and die is all we can do,
Our children deserve the right to live in peace,
Not die on your battlefield,
May God give us the strength to carry on.

CHILDREN OF WAR

I cry for my children they suffer through no fault of their own.
They ask me where is daddy and when will he be coming home.
He will be back soon I tell them,
They fall asleep to dream of his return,
I know in my heart he will not be coming home but I must keep their dreams alive.
My children will grow up without their daddy,
For now, he will live on in their dreams.
As they sleep my tears cascade down my face,
The tears are dry before they wake.
My heart is broken yet I must stay strong for them,
All we have now is each other,
May God give me strength to carry on for them.

DUST OF BATTLE

The dust has settled, the blood has dried, men cry no more,
The sound of war has gone,
Birds sing out once again in the treetops,
The fighting has finished the killing stopped,
Dead lay in the fields their duty done,
Why were we fighting and who won this war?
Families wait for their loved ones to return,
Many will not come home they rest where they fell,
Crowds line the streets and cheer with joy,
As soldiers march with pride for all to see,
We won the war at last they say,
Those left behind will never know.

MY LOVING DOG

A faithful partner was my loving dog,
Seeking only to give me his love when I needed it most,
Asking for no reward except a pat or gentle stroke,
Always by my side watching my every move,
Following me wherever I would go,
A trusty friend who did not speak but understood my every word,
My loving dog, my partner he was the best,
I miss him every day and now I walk alone,
I'm thankful for the many years of joy and happiness we shared,
Rest in peace my old friend.

SOLDIER'S LAST WORDS

On the battlefield a brave soldier lay wounded,
Please help me I'm dying he pleads,
I want to see my mother and father again,
As he looks into the eyes of a medic, he asks will I be OK,
The medic replies you will be fine knowing that the soldier is dying,
If I die please tell my mother and father I love them,
Please don't forget to tell them that's all I ask of you,
In his pouch is found a picture of his mother and father,
On the back is written, "Stay Safe and Come Home Soon. Love Mum and Dad xxx".
So many soldiers never had the chance to say their last goodbyes.

I AM WHO I AM

I may look and act different than most, that I know,
Some people stare at me and turn away,
I'm not a monster from the deep,
The hurt I feel is hidden deep inside,
They know not why I am this way,
I've accepted the way I am that I can't change,
Life is good to me, I'm happy in my little world,
I do not need sympathy or pity,
A friendly greeting, a nice smile or helping hand would make my day,
All I ask is to be treated with kindness and respect,
Please accept me I AM WHO I AM.

CALL TO DUTY

In times of need they stepped up,
They joined the cause to fight for our freedom,
From villages and towns across the land they came,
They travelled to war on ships and planes,
To strange lands they never knew before,
Mates and friends together they went,
Not knowing what lay ahead,
Bravely fighting side by side until the bitter end,
For many their final resting place we know not where,
They are our heroes who gave their todays,
For our tomorrows,
We shall always remember their sacrifice.

BAD DAY

My bad day is not so bad,
When I think of those who have no food to eat,
My bad day is not so bad,
When I see people sleeping in the street,
My bad day is not so bad,
When I see an ambulance rush by,
My bad day is not so bad,
When I see those refugees on TV,
My bad day is not so bad,
So, when all is lost and you feel down,
Look around,
Think of those who are having a bad day,
Your day has just got brighter.

FATHER'S FOOTSTEPS

With tears in her eyes
mummy told us last night,
Daddy won't be coming home,
I need to be alone I said,
Time to think what I must do,
I'm the man of the house now,
Taking care of mummy and my little brother and sister,
That's what I must do,
Filling in his footsteps I'll do my best,
I miss him so much I always will,
For him I'll be strong and take charge,
In his memory I'll stand proud and strong,
The love he gave me will last forever,
I would give anything to hold his hand just one more time,
I can see his smile and feel his last hug,
In my dreams he will be alive forever,
I am a proud son of a fallen hero.

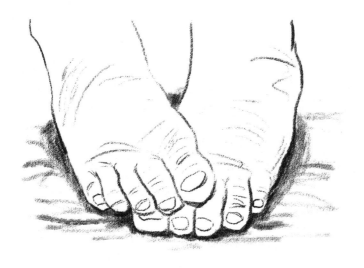

MY FEET ARE COLD

My feet are cold I have no socks or shoes to wear,
It's snowing outside but I can't go out to play,
I sometimes wear my sister's sandals while she sleeps,
Father carries me on his shoulders when it's wet outside,
Mother makes soup that helps to keep me warm,
My friend I used to play with died yesterday,
His mother gave me his shoes,
I am looking forward to the summer sun,
When my feet will be warm again.

THE WAVES

Sitting on the sand dunes listening to the waves,
Watching the sea get closer to shore,
Time has no meaning for the sea it does what it wants,
The tide ebbs and flows the day away,
Waves continually washing against the rocks,
As the sea makes its way to shore,
Children waiting eagerly to play and paddle in the waves,
Seagulls glide overhead in the summer breeze,
Like white dots in the distant sky as they fly away,
Cries of the gulls are muffled by the noise of the waves,
The warm summer breeze softly blowing on my face,
Breathing the warm sea air rejuvenates my sole,
My mind drifts into emptiness as I close my eyes,
The troubles of the day are all washed away.

TRANQUIL COUNTRYSIDE

The valley and distant hills shine in the early morning sun,
The fields are all shades of green like a patch work quilt spread out across the land.
Hedges, fences and stone walls twist and turn separating fields.
Cows and sheep wander aimlessly in the pasture grazing as they go.
Dark clouds and thunderstorms creep over the hills bringing rainy days.
Clouds of mist roll across the land covering rivers and lakes,
The countryside so tranquil and beautiful at its best,
Hike along the trails or walk by the rivers,
Enjoy the beautiful English countryside.

VILLAGE LIFE

The village school playground is alive with children playing games,
Cows and sheep pass unnoticed wandering through the fields,
Wildflowers in the hedgerows bloom with bright colors,
Trees give shade from the summer sun,
Rabbits and hedgehogs scurry through the tall grass into their dens,
The river runs free with crystal-clear water snaking its way through the village,
Birds flutter above in the treetops singing their songs,
Seasons come and go but village life doesn't change,
Life is slow and meaningful as it's always been,
Village folk are happy and contented to be left alone,
So, keep the hustle and bustle of the big city lights,
Village life's for me.

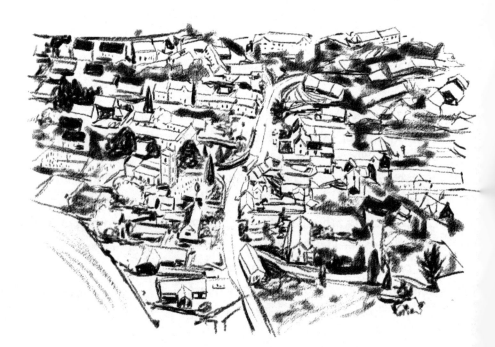

SUFFERING IN SILENCE

Hidden from friends for fear of shame,
Silently suffering the torment and abuse,
Feeling frightened and depressed I struggle on,
Heartache brings sadness that's dragging me down,
Watching my family slowly torn apart,
Is more than I can bear,
Who is this monster I'm living with?
The person I loved now fear and hate,
I'm searching for answers before it's too late,
To pluck up courage and contact a friend,
Provide me strength at this critical time,
With love and support I will see it through,
No more torment and abuse I'm free at last,
A bright new future is waiting for me,
My head held high and smile on my face,
Those years of heartache are lost in the past.

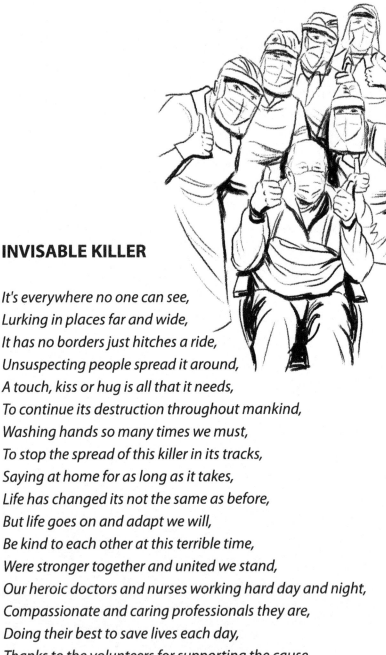

INVISABLE KILLER

It's everywhere no one can see,
Lurking in places far and wide,
It has no borders just hitches a ride,
Unsuspecting people spread it around,
A touch, kiss or hug is all that it needs,
To continue its destruction throughout mankind,
Washing hands so many times we must,
To stop the spread of this killer in its tracks,
Saying at home for as long as it takes,
Life has changed its not the same as before,
But life goes on and adapt we will,
Be kind to each other at this terrible time,
Were stronger together and united we stand,
Our heroic doctors and nurses working hard day and night,
Compassionate and caring professionals they are,
Doing their best to save lives each day,
Thanks to the volunteers for supporting the cause,
The British spirit is still alive and well,
Brighter days are ahead be British and stick together.

OUR CHOICE

Our rivers are running dry as never before,
Others are clogged and contaminated by waste,
Oceans are being fouled by plastic we throw,
Millions have no clean water to drink through no fault of their own,
The planet is dying and save it we must,
The next generation deserves better than this,
Its never too later to save what is left,
Looking our children in the eye we can say,
We are leaving you clean water but there is much more to do,
To clean up our rivers and oceans will take time,
So, continue this effort long after we're gone,
The choice we have is not difficult to make,
Do nothing and let the environment die,
Or be responsible people and clean up the mess,
THAT IS OUR CHOICE.

SOLDIERS' JOURNEYS END

The war is over we fight no more,
Wounds are dressed and home they go,
Lay down your gun's you men of war,
Bullets have no targets anymore,
Let the dead now rest in peace,
They have reached their journey's end,
Young and old lay side by side,
Travelling together through the clouds of mist,
Reaching journey's end before their time,
Peace at last they do find,
Flowers upon their grave wither in time,
Their names are written in stone and will never fade,
A soldier's journey ended here.

TIME

Tick tock, tick tock,
Ever moving forward,
Never looking back always forward,
Controlling lives,
Tick tock, tick tock,
One more second, one more minute, one more hour,
One more day one more night,
Tick tock, tick tock,
Always on your mind,
Ten minutes more, don't be late,
What time is the next train,
You must be there on time,
Tick tock, tick tock,
Time waits for no one.

OLD AGE

Although I am old and slowing down,
You bet, I am still alive and well,
Done my bit along the way,
No regrets I've got to say,
My mind is sharp but slowing down,
Memories of the past I still recall,
Forgetful at times my children say,
I now cherish life the simple way,
Happiness and laughter are important to me,
Life is too short at my stage in life,
One day at a time is what I will do,
Forget old age It is just a number they say,
Live for the present and think of the past,
You have arrived so cherish what is left.

THEY AND I

I live in a warm dry house with electricity,
They live in a cold damp tent,
I sleep in a bed with pillows, sheets and blankets,
They sleep on the floor with United Nations High Commission
for Refugees (UNHCR) polythene bags for blankets,
I get up and have a choice of food for breakfast,
They get up and if lucky have food,
I go to work to support my family,
They stay have no work and stay in a camp,
I have a choice to eat at home or go to a restaurant,
They have no choice and live off food aid,
I am free to travel,
They are restricted to living in a refugee camp,
THEY would give anything to be free and safe like I.

CHILDREN SUFFER

Babies crying in their mother's arms,
As they run through the bombed-out streets,
Weaving In and out of rubble they run as fast as they can,
Afraid and looking for shelter somewhere to hide.
Bullets and bombs exploding all around,
Families with children run hand in hand,
Exhausted and tired stopping to rest,
Children are frightened and crying out loud,
Too young to understand the meaning of war,
Their mother comforts them the best she can,
Facing hardships together one day at a time,
Caught up in battle through no fault of their own,
Children of war your sad faces tell it all,
Your cries and tears are too much to bear,
No child deserves to grow up in pain,
You are the future we hope and pray,
That one day soon your life will change,
Finding a bright new future with happiness along the way.

FEATHERED FRIENDS

So many birds too many to count,
Small birds with tiny wings flying all around,
Large birds we know and see them every day,
Calling out their message from woods and beyond,
Waking us each morning singing their songs,
Morning has broken like the first morning, black bird
has spoken like the first bird,
Perch on our fences, electric wires and roofs,
Watching over us as they do,
Without them life would be dull just not the same,
Protect their environment so that future generations
will enjoy the sight and sounds of birds.

FOOD FOR THOUGHT

Most of us have enough food to eat,
Yet millions of people around the world go hungry every single day,
Many people starve to death and that is a shame,
Do not waste your food and throw it away,
While others are desperate for food to eat,
No one should go hungry in this land of ours,
We must make sure that today and every day,
Food is available for everyone.
No child should cry and go to bed hungry,
No senior citizen should have to beg for food,
We must make sure that today and every day,
No one goes hungry,
Please donate to your local food bank,
No matter how small every donation helps,
Someone will be grateful.

DEATH OF A DICTATOR

You deserve to die for torturing and killing millions of your people,
Your people suffered, you have blood on your hands,
Your people lived in poverty and misery while you lived in luxury,
Your people died of starvation while you ate the finest food,
You stole their money to buy houses in foreign lands,
You used their money to buy expensive cars,
Your citizens begged for food and money to survive,
Good riddance you tyrant you should have died long ago,
We need no more dictators in this land of ours,
We suffered for years under your rule,
Now that you are gone, we can rebuild our lives,
Make our country great as it was before,
Sweep away memories of the past,
Making a brighter future for our children,
Dictator may you rot in hell.

BOY SOLDIER

They took me out of school,
To fight in a war,
Gave me a gun and taught me to kill,
Follow their orders I was told to do,
I lived like an animal no thoughts of my own,
Killing women and children that did me no harm,
They were bodies not people just cast aside,
Seeing death as I did trouble me not,
The fighting has ended, and I am going home,
Going back to school to learn what I can,
Forget the past and try to move on,
The pain that I feel will be difficult to mend,
I have my whole life ahead of me now,
So, the dark days of yesterday I must try to forget.

MY COMPANION

My furry friend brings me comfort when I am down,
Quietly wandering around my home,
Curling up next to me often brings joy,
Asking for nothing yet faithful as can be,
Purring with affection it knows what I need,
No mice in my house they have been chased away,
Silently slipping away for days at a time,
Returning hungry and bedraggled creeping back in,
Running and jumping around the house as before,
Taking its place on the back of the chair,
Looking out of the window at people passing by,
Always around so I am never alone,
A companion that brings me comfort and joy,
That is my companion my feline friend.

TECHNOLOGY

Technology is changing the way that we live,
Spending hours on computers, phones and more,
Communicating on apps is the new norm,
Rushing around with a phone to one ear,
Typing a message while walking around,
Bumping into people and not giving a damn,
It is so important to get that message away,
Internet options confuses us all,
Hackers and scammers trying to break in,
Locking our computers for hours at a time,
Frustration takes over when passwords are not found,
A new one is needed before we are locked out,
Calling for help to get a fix,
Chatting with a foreigner who you cannot understand,
Buying a new computer to get ahead of the game,
By the time you get home a new model is out,
Technology syndrome is stressful enough,
Therapists now offer a treatment for this,
I am old school and been trying my best,
Learning this technology is too much for me now,
I am ditching it all and going back to the pen,
Leaving technology where it belongs,
With the next generation who need it the most.

ON THE EDGE

Our world is facing disaster it is a race against time,
Ice packs are melting at an alarming rate,
Carbon monoxide is fouling the air,
Temperatures are rising causing a drought,
Millions of people have no water to drink,
Harm to the environment is continuing today,
We cannot undo the damage that is done,
We can stop further decline by addressing the problems
before it is too late,
Stop using plastic and recycle all waste,
Green energy will help clean the environment too,
By reducing emissions that is fouling the air,
Our landfills are contaminated with toxic waste,
Fouling the ground for centuries to come,
With global warming under control,
The environment will be cleaner than before,
Making our planet a better place to live.

SAVE OUR OCEANS

Our oceans are refreshing and important to us,
Things are fast changing and out of control,
Contaminated and clogged with plastic and waste,
Oceans are being suffocated dying a slow death,
Coral reefs are dying and soon will be gone,
Over-fishing is taking its toll,
Fish that were plentiful can no longer be found,
Dead fish and plastic are washed up on our shores,
Contaminating beaches where our children play,
How much longer can we let this go on,
Responsible nations must do their bit,
Take immediate action to clean up this mess,
Protect and preserve the world oceans,
Making a healthy environment where marine life can live.

1948 UNIVERSAL DECLARATION OF HUMAN RIGHTS WE THE PEOPLES OF THE UNITED NATIONS DETERMINED

- to save succeeding generations from the scourge of war, which twice in our lifetime has brought untold sorrow to mankind, and

- to reaffirm faith in fundamental human rights, in the dignity and worth of the human person, in the equal rights of men and women and of nations large and small, and

- to establish conditions under which justice and respect for the obligations arising from treaties and other sources of international law can be maintained, and

- to promote social progress and better standards of life in larger freedom,

AND FOR THESE ENDS

- to practice tolerance and live together in peace with one another as good neighbours, and

- to unite our strength to maintain international peace and security, and

- to ensure, by the acceptance of principles and the institution of methods, that armed force shall not be used, save in the common interest, and

- to employ international machinery for the promotion of the economic and social advancement of all peoples.

The Universal Declaration of Human Rights:

1. We are all free and equal. We are all born free. We all have our own thoughts and ideas. We should all be treated in the same way.

2. Don't discriminate. These rights belong to everybody, whatever our differences.

3. The right to life. We all have the right to life, and to live in freedom and safety.

4. No slavery - past and present. Nobody has any right to make us a slave. We cannot make anyone our slave.

5. No Torture. Nobody has any right to hurt us or to torture us.

6. We all have the same right to use the law. I am a person just like you!

7. We are all protected by the law. The law is the same for everyone. It must treat us all fairly.

8. Fair treatment by fair courts. We can all ask for the law to help us when we are not treated fairly.

9. No unfair detainment. Nobody has the right to put us in prison without a good reason and keep us there, or to send us away from our country.

10. The right to trial. If we are put on trial this should be in public. The people who try us should not let anyone tell them what to do.

11. Innocent until proven guilty. Nobody should be blamed for doing something until it is proven. When people say we did a bad thing we have the right to show it is not true.

12. The right to privacy. Nobody should try to harm our good name. Nobody has the right to come into our home, open our letters or bother us or our family without a good reason.

13. Freedom to move. We all have the right to go where we want in our own country and to travel as we wish.

14. The right to asylum. If we are frightened of being badly treated in our own country, we all have the right to run away to another country to be safe.

15. The right to a nationality. We all have the right to belong to a country.

16. Marriage and family. Every grown-up has the right to marry and have a family if they want to. Men and women have the same rights when they are married, and when they are separated.

17. Your own things. Everyone has the right to own things or share them. Nobody should take our things from us without a good reason.

18. Freedom of thought. We all have the right to believe in what we want to believe, to have a religion, or to change it if we want.

19. Free to say what you want. We all have the right to make up our own minds, to think what we like, to say what we think, and to share our ideas with other people.

20. Meet where you like. We all have the right to meet our friends and to work together in peace to defend our rights. Nobody can make us join a group if we don't want to.

21. The right to democracy. We all have the right to take part in the government of our country. Every grown-up should be allowed to choose their own leaders.

22. The right to social security. We all have the right to affordable housing, medicine, education, and child care, enough money to live on and medical help if we are ill or old.

23. Workers' rights. Every grown-up has the right to do a job, to a fair wage for their work, and to join a trade union.

24. The right to play. We all have the right to rest from work and to relax.

25. A bed and some food. We all have the right to a good life. Mothers and children, people who are old, unemployed or disabled, and all people have the right to be cared for.

26. The right to education. Education is a right. Primary school should be free. We should learn about the United Nations and how to get on with others. Our parents can choose what we learn.

27. Culture and copyright. Copyright is a special law that protects one's own artistic creations and writings; others cannot make copies without permission. We all have the right to our own way of life and to enjoy the good things that "art," science and learning bring.

28. A free and fair world. There must be proper order so we can all enjoy rights and freedoms in our own country and all over the world.

29. Our responsibilities. We have a duty to other people, and we should protect their rights and freedoms.

30. Nobody can take away these rights and freedoms from us.

List provided by Youth For Human Rights International, adapted and simplified from the 1948 Universal Declaration of Human Rights

Printed in Great Britain
by Amazon

23797292R00030